INHERITED SHADOWS

INHERITED SHADOWS

ELIAS HARTLEY

CONTENTS

First Printing, 2024

CHAPTER 1

Introduction

Rahhal's essay about inherited family pain locates the start of her inscribed trauma in her doubly exilic, Paterson, New Jersey, roots. Here, she tells her grandparents' story of origin, an archive of hasty marriages, and their only son, her father, a man troubled throughout his life by his upbringing and the negative, probably abusive, influence of his parents. At its best, her father's wrenching beauty results in a good musical note, some passing recognition of her talents, a fleeting insight and aphorism, an emotional openness to life's living dichotomies, and a lifelong constrained anger against his own parents, against his own requirements and his own exile. What remain as lasting quality marks from father to daughter are deep shadows that follow her entire life as lingering ghosts from lives that she never partook of, shadows that seemed determined to latch on for the hurtful times.

Inherited Shadows: Breaking the Cycle of Family Trauma will explore Rahhal's experience with inherited pain and the paths away from it. At the heart of her essay is an analysis of and response to Octavia Butler's Parable of the Sower and Parable of the Talents. Readers should expect an intimate look at the lasting traumatic effects of trauma on families, a study of speculative, post-apocalyptic fiction, the examination of ways of coping with inherited pain, and attempts to conceptualize an end to internalized wars. The essay moves from a family story to literary and psychological theorizing to offer what Rahhal calls "a fantasy that causes me pain, that I spend so much energy on." Her essay is an illustration of the connections a rigorous study of the literature of trauma, both familial and collective, can provoke from a personal perspective and vantage point.

Understanding Family Trauma

Family trauma is a complex issue that has far-reaching implications in the personal lives of many individuals. From substance use disorder to physical and emotional neglect, the trauma that takes place in one generation often finds itself repeated in the following generations. Because family trauma is often pegged to certain behaviors of a familial role model, these behaviors continue on through the family line, solidifying themselves in family traditions and expectations and subsequently solidifying their negative effects on individuals. This article aims to improve understanding of the issue while also communicating the message that it is possible to break the insidious cycles of generational trauma.

The psychologist Murray Bowen introduced the concept of the Family Projection Process, which suggests that issues of self - such as unresolved trauma, stressful experiences, and chronic emotional vulnerabilities - can become projected onto a child in a process that can weaken the boundaries of the family system. Weak boundaries result in multiple processes that researchers generally label as enmeshment. This promotion of a narrow and illusory sense of self shows the cyclical nature of family trauma and the importance placed on removing enmeshment and establishing healthy boundaries with the understanding that these family roles are part of a generational issue, not just that of the individual.

CHAPTER 2

The Impact of Inherited Shadows

Excerpted from Inherited Shadows: Breaking the Cycle of Family Trauma by Laura Lynn LaPointe, PhD. Available September 2022 from New Harbinger Publications.

Inherited shadows are unconscious, historical patterns of loss, grief, resilience, and healing that are passed from one generation to the next. These hidden legacies can play out in our bodies, relationships, and behaviors, changing our lives before we are even born. Just as there is a top-down therapy—psychotherapy for individuals in which the clinician explores a person's childhood to understand who they are—an intergenerational perspective has a bottom-up and top-down component that involves understanding relational dynamics and the family's historical circumstances. We develop in the present as an intersection of our past and the people who raised us who were raised by others. Our families are the first smaller culture we are born into. There are shared illusions and absurd realities we absorb first, simply because they are presented to us as "normal." These manifest as implicit expectations, including losing a parent through chronic mental illness or acting out, suppressing "negative" emotions, hiding family trauma, or feeling responsible to manage everyone's discomfort.

Many people identify that the implicit family expectations they make part of growing up in their families of origin continue to affect them, even when they have begun the healing work of delineating where they come from. For example, one's self-concept is initially absorbed from family members. This is the arena or the prism in which, historically, our personalities develop. Additionally, a concept developed in the research on families of Holocaust survivors is the survivor personality in general: how you live in the world will be shaped by personal, social, familial, and tribal legacy of being targeted in a mass traumatic event. Families who have experienced atrocity live with an artifact of grief, even if unnamed or unmarked. If sewing patterns of survival are passed down alongside attachment patterns, the worldview is intergenerationally self-validating and maintained by shared historical and current danger. The family legacy is developed through unifying around unspeakable experiences as experienced and/or felt. A combination of intergenerationally absorbed coping and our existential threat positions are what constitutes these Unconscious Historical Inheritance Legacies (UHILs).

Psychological Effects

The research of the effects of these traumas has shown that they have a huge psychological impact. "These messages are not an unfounded fear or the product of a cultural pessimism. Evidence is mounting that certain types of early adversity can significantly damage a child's developing brain, impacting the child's mental health and his capacity to learn." This is not only the result of acts of abuse or overt violence, such as can occur in alcoholic or abusive families, but also from more subtle forms of parental neglect. For children of parents who are emotionally absent through having unresolved issues themselves (e.g. childhood traumas), can have even more marked psychological effects. It has also been shown that even if the parent has later resolved these problems, their child will experience less psychological distress, which suggests that the shadow is being inherited in some way.

Trauma usually leads to children adopting excessive guilt. When the trauma involves an adult they love, a child who knows the dreadful thing that has been done to them often judges that the adult would not do it unless he had acted badly; has, in fact, encouraged and brought it on. Often the child feels they could have prevented it from happening. They may be similarly unreasonably guilty by identifying with the perpetrator, such as thinking secretly they are as bad as they are or could become as bad as the perpetrator. So rather than hating a violent or incestuous father (or a toxic mother), a child often 'splits off' the painful feelings and admires the perpetrator. The most accessible parent day and says they will become just like their father or mother (none of us really do, but more on that below). If that admired parent is scary and violent, the children will do their best to deny the evidence that this admired parent is as violent a child abuser. A child who has had their spirits broken will over time build protective mechanisms around their hearts to avoid feeling their own emotions.

CHAPTER 3

Identifying and Acknowledging Family Trauma

Trauma is insidious, invisible, and multigenerational. When the effects of past trauma are carried down through generations, we refer to it as family trauma, generational trauma, inherited trauma, or transgenerational trauma. The fact of the matter is that many of us had difficult, abusive, or otherwise severely disruptive parents, and until that is identified, acknowledged, and something positive is done to break the cycle, bitterness will go on and on.

Signs of family trauma can present themselves in many different fashions. Some people can clearly recall from a young age being groomed for family expectations, while others show resilience to those expectations. According to psychologists, childhood trauma can manifest in the following ways that can result in an unnatural character load in later life: smiling in various atmospheres, bragging about one's self or family, exuding excessive pride about physical abilities, power, showing off knowledge, gossiping, bullying and encouraging infighting, or denigrating others (including family members). If any of us recognize our own family using these tactics, it may be worthwhile to identify the type of family condition we have.

Recognizing Patterns

For many people, the "sins of the fathers" are not only a way of acknowledging that one generation tends to follow in the footsteps of the previous one, but also that the weaknesses, traumas, and even vices of one generation tend to assert themselves in the lives of the next. One might therefore regard an exploration of "family traumas" or "inherited shadows" as an attempt to find a new way of understanding the old tradition of acknowledging that the fruit does not fall far from the tree. However, what follows in this document, collected from research and from first-person narratives, is also designed to help us ask how we feel or relate to these patterns when we observe them, or when they are pointed out to us. The article will focus on recognizing patterns related to trauma and will also provide activities and questions for "at home" exploration.

Themes and Behaviors Trauma may be reproduced during and across generations. The traumatic scene and its themes can be understood to serve as a key decipher for the understanding and recognition of inherited shadows, namely, to recognize signs of inherited trauma, look for problems of boundary maintenance, difficulties in establishing physical and psychological boundaries, and thereby difficulties in managing relationships. Trauma is also implicated in relationships with time: ellipses, leaps, fragments, repetitions, losses, and crises are all recognized as potential features of inherited trauma.

CHAPTER 4

Interpersonal Relationships and Family Trauma

Interpersonal relationships, both with family members and with others, are fundamentally changed by family trauma. The trauma becomes a quintessential focus, and yet it so often remains unspoken. It becomes the proverbial elephant in the room, a secret well-hidden behind tears, anger, and silence. The limits of family members' ability to communicate devastate their ability to forge healthy, trusting relationships with one another as well as with those outside the home. People who grew up in trauma-laden families often fear love, believing it to be untrustworthy at best and dangerous at worst. Whether overtly or subconsciously, they find ways to sabotage any offers of love that come their way. In this way, the consequences of our childhood programming can shadow us throughout our lives.

The importance of healthy communication in the family dynamic can't be overstated. The impact of childhood experiences on one's adult self cannot be undone, but communication about the trauma can help to heal both children and adults. It will give children a way to integrate events in their lives that they simply can't understand. It's imperative for children to know that regardless of what happened, their world won't turn completely upside down. For the adults, communication about the traumatic event reduces shame and brings back control from their past to the present. Finally, communication is where change begins, and offering children an alternate language provides hope and opportunity for a positive re-scripting of their stories.

Communication Strategies

Communication strategies. In the context of family trauma, one should rely on communication that is clear (emphasizing the information you wish to convey), honest (admitting what you don't know and why decisions are made or not made), and direct (talking plainly). When communicating with children, a parent/guardian/counselor can follow a four-step model: 1) Notice the signs of trauma (since problems associated with trauma are easily mistaken for other problems), 2) ask direct questions about how the child is coping (prod: do you feel like you're having a hard time?; ask open-ended questions: how have you been doing at school? or just ask: tell me what is it like for you), 3) help the child talk (triggering topics: discuss what it's like living in your neighborhood these days or what do you think the war in Iraq is doing to us?), and 4) listen (even if a child doesn't want to talk, it can be helpful to know he/she won't be judged or criticized if he/she ever does want to talk). Finally, show understanding, empathy, and respect for the child's coping strategies.

Given the complexities of social etiquette, communicating well requires practice and self-reflection, as well as active engagement and interest. While willing to be savvy, a communicator must remain open to increasing knowledge of communication strategies. People can demonstrate caring to one another by clearly providing necessary information, and they can simultaneously mitigate interpersonal struggles by sparing confessions of subjective doubt, frustration, anxiety, and despair. Oddly, struggling communicators may begin to show less concern for the appropriateness of a message and more focus on making themselves heard - despite the impropriety of their topic or complaint. Oddly, these communicated feelings may "give voice to" known and unknown complaints that inadvertently extend beyond the speaker.

CHAPTER 5

Healing and Recovery

The first step toward healing from adversity is learning to recognize how your body registers that harm. It's pretty difficult to make any changes to your system until you have some knowledge of where you stand. Those who are fortunate to have not experienced this level of adversity may not be able to understand or relate to it. As a result, they tend to minimize the impact that those experiences have on survivors and can sometimes cause more harm in the process.

Over time, the body will begin to feel a bit better. The mind will start to clear and then what? Once healing is underway and the crisis is over, it is time to think about what can help people recover and what can be done to help prevent future traumas. What works for one person may not work for the next and most of the time people need a combination of different treatments and care. That being said, there are many therapists and doctors trained specifically in trauma treatments that can help those who have experienced traumas. In fact, there are many groups, different places, organizations and programs that offer trauma treatments and therapies to help. This section's goal is to provide a look at some different treatment approaches that have evidence to show that they are effective for survivors of adversities.

Therapeutic Approaches

As family trauma is engineered by traumatic experiences, be it at a personal or familial level, it is caused or triggered by relationships that occur within a family context. The discussion thus far has been based on healing and recovery, especially how to address parental mental health and substance use issues. One may see these approaches as part of the healing and becoming of families because they can unburden and reassign roles in generational cycles of trauma, thereby creating a new history for the next generation of children. But the question remains how and if people can untangle the knotted histories of their lives and those of their families, and how to engage and witness interventions.

There are many paths to navigate, and in working with families who are traumatized sometimes it is through developing and working with an innovative integrative or multimodal model to gain a new start or understanding or angle or therapeutic peace which is necessary. Trauma-focused therapies, especially when addressing single incident forms of trauma, for example post-incident stress, can work within a time-limited, incident-specific model, frequently using methods that work across a spectrum of trauma, e.g. Flash Technique, Eye Movement Desensitization and Reprocessing or EMDR, and Narrative Methods. Family Narrative Therapy can help an entire family develop a new coherent version of their generational story, freeing it from the tyranny of a traumatic past. Working with any one of these perspectives may, can and will support an integrated individual and family counseling model.

CHAPTER 6

Preventive Measures and Breaking the Cycle

Historically, social work practice has been crisis-oriented and intervention-focused. The research in this study, however, explores prevention and/or proactive measures. Working with the field of social services allows us to not only change the lives of these children but also the lives of their unborn children. It provides us with the opportunity to be part of breaking the cycle of family trauma. At least 38 states have plus one educational programs to help children from alcoholic families. Some programs begin as early as kindergarten and progress with the children. Other Plus one programs gear their services more towards the middle-school and high school age population. Other services such as 12 Step or self-help programs for older children and adults seem to be the successful part of addiction intervention. Arresting or hospitalizing a parent is seen to be a major rupturing force in the child's life, particularly when coupled with the services given to the affected children.

Some educational programs also have the materials available for the caregivers. Other programs offer the support and care for the caregivers. It is proposed that every family involved in a substance abuse presentation of services must have some follow-up, monitoring and/or family support. It is essential to break the cycle; the gradual interventions alone would indicate whether the prevention aspect was gaining momentum. It is mentioned here that foster care intervention is proposed as a temporary measure. Thus, once the immediate crisis of a family is over, there is potential reduction in family length of stay and possible savings for the state intervention.

Educational Programs

The potential usefulness of preventative measures is explored during consultation. Education is one of the easiest and most readily available preventative measures and has been used with many groups who might come into contact with affected descendants, for example:

- Healthcare professionals - Teachers - The police force/deal with social care issues - Religious organisations joining with Spiritual Care and afterlife organisations

Educational programmes have been run attracting up to 400 delegates at a conference around Mental Health and the Aftermath of High Stakes Lifesaving within an emergency driven organisation and in excess of 400 for the Prison Service. The generic nature of education allows for long-term sustainability, those attending have also included descendants (UK and Belgium) plus various survivors. The aim of these programmes is to provide information to the practitioners, giving an educational model that can be utilised in day to day practice, for example promoting discussion to consider different, potential, personalised needs of those indirectly affected. Greater knowledge and empathy would then enable support to be tailored more closely to the individual family, especially when in the acute stages of diagnosis, and possibly prevent family trees from being blighted or have the potential for negative effects in the future.

Educational programmes have also been shared with children and young descendants at a summer school focusing mainly on building resilience, different populations have been evaluated and one to one support is being developed for those more traumatised children. Increased knowledge is associated with reducing the potential impact, breaking the connection and cycle of the inherited shadows.

CHAPTER 7

Cultural and Historical Context

In the American psyche, the notion of family trauma or dysfunction has long been of interest. For example, the concept of the 'sins of the father' extending to impact the lives of the children was first popularized in the Old Testament - and remains relevant today. This perspective allows for a broader study of generational trauma. The term 'intergenerational transmission of trauma' was coined by Mendel in 1947, investigating second-generation Holocaust survivors. Today, this concept and its related phenomena are studied more broadly as generational trauma, branching into a variety of different societal and cultural implications. For example, Japanese have long used the term 'karma of the third generation' to describe such transgenerational patterns, while the United States of America has long been operating and responding to the 'cycle of poverty.'

The term 'generational trauma' is relatively modern, garnering increased credence after the telling of familial stories and personal epigenetic studies began surfacing. Mainstream interest in the concept grew after the publication of The Body Keeps the Score, lending generational psychological trauma additional scholarly interest as well. As the scholarly understanding of a collective epigenetic inheritance grows, it also becomes increasingly important to discuss. Thus, this paper aims to conceptually define generational of familial trauma and contextualize this phenomenon within the scope of generational dialogue. Then, it will describe an emerging educational roundtable designed to non-exhaustively discuss individual interactions with inherited shadows, aiming to break the cycle of generational or familial trauma.

Generational Trauma

It is not enough to assess the individual context in the course of therapy, or even just the cultural context of the individual. An important starting point is the historical context, which may, for example, provide an explanation for why a problem, though created in one generation, has become overwhelming for the next. It is thus helpful to embark on a genealogical exploration in an attempt to understand family 'myth' and collective history. There is a distinction between collective (war, famine) which may impact society more generally and personal. This part, however, will deal with the idea of events which were felt personally. This idea has its roots in humanism and the development of individualism in the eighteenth century which sees effects of events being transmitted as a result of the construction of self. This part will be useful in work with both individuals and couples. The idea of generational scapegoating which is transferred over generations as a result of never resolved grievances legitimizes a flow, however negative, being maintained across members.

Retro-homeostasis, i.e., a resting point reached after a tumultuous period, and which maintains the wounds at a certain level to protect the link between members, can be creative. Systemically speaking, retro-homeostasis is thus a homeostasis allowing a kind of homeostatic relationship to the catastrophic. When the 'influx of danger' from the not acknowledged disaster (NAD) is too great, the family must be protected by formulating certain fundamental identity injunctions, based on genealogy/genealogy and NAD story transmission, honoring, so safeguarding the integrity of previous generations, often at cost of the post-trauma dynamics.

CHAPTER 8

Conclusion

In this report, we have delved into the mechanisms of development and transmission of family trauma. We have described diverse family traumas, namely, war violence and domestic violence, and their impact on parents' ability to care for and bond with their child. War trauma was investigated in families originating from the country of former Yugoslavia. Country context was given, and the mental health status of the adults from these families was described. Families with a complex pattern of war-related traumatization, parental loss, and interparental domestic violence were compared with other refugee families. In the third section, we discussed the correlation between the pediatric status of posttraumatic stress disorder and psychiatric disturbances (PTSD-PC) and domestic violence.

Moving forward in healing. In the introduction, we raised the question if it's possible to break the cycle of transmitted adversity and family trauma to the next generation. In the three sections that followed, it was made clear that it is not through silent avoidance one can heal a family. If families do not overcome the wall of shame, if they stay silent in their box of fear and avoidance, they cannot benefit from interventions and treatments. In silence and shame, the intergenerational legacy hides. When social, health, or mental health organizations refuse to investigate family relationships and life stories, they don't only potentiate the burden on the carer. It depends on them if the parent carers become the victim who wants to shout: "someone take away my child" or if they become the survivor who is singing: "Do you hear the people sing, singing the song of angry men?" Instead of just the carer, it becomes a whole family journey.

Moving Forward in Healing

The damage caused by traumatic events can last for centuries. The awareness and visibility of racism, sexism, and other forms of oppression bring forth emotional shadows within our psyches and in our societies. Inherited shadows have the power to control our lives from distances we do not always notice or understand. However, growing our consciousness of these shadows through history, adaptations, and within our families, we can begin moving forward in a manner of healing. Naming these truths is a contemporary disarming of the buried past's effect on our present and future. The biological, emotional, psychological, and most importantly, analytical inheritances of trauma keep the damaging past alive across the generations. Identifying and naming family trauma can give us hope and power to break the invisible chains, to let go and forgive those who've passed on our shame, and step into the new light of healing and connection.

Breaking free of the trauma that comes to us as a burden of previous generations is not only necessary for our personal and greater collective psyches to thrive, but it allows for love, hope, and joy to flow through our veins uncontaminated. Acknowledging that trauma spans from the individual to a national focus point, as well as its severity and how pearly or sinister it may express itself, family trauma also ebbs in and out and through one person to the next as an unspoken, lived shadow. The good news is that by tracing back these hidden stories, we are no longer doomed to repeat them. Instead, we can tell them differently with new choices, expanding our identity beyond the narrow tribal and genetic field.

www.ingramcontent.com/pod-product-compliance
Lightning Source LLC
LaVergne TN
LVHW090336210926
848480LV00004B/1441
9798330395040